I0570307

THE BEHAVIOR TOOLBOX

A Guidebook for Parents
(With Strategies and Tracking Sheets)

ALANA SIMPSON

Copyright © 2024 Alana Simpson.

All Rights Reserved. This book contains material protected under International and Federal Copyright Laws and Treaties. Any unauthorized reprint or use of this material is prohibited. No part of this book may be reproduced or transmitted in any form or by any means, electronic or mechanical, including photocopying, recording, or by any information storage and retrieval system without express written permission from the author/publisher.

ISBN: 979-8-9909817-0-6 (Hardcover)
ISBN: 979-8-9909817-1-3 (Paperback)
ISBN: 979-8-9909817-2-0 (Ebook)

DEDICATION

I'm dedicating this book to my mom, Janis; dad, Clayton; and grandmothers, Denny and Hattie. These four people shaped me into the person I am today. They have been my greatest teachers; they taught me everything I know about never giving up, even in the face of adversity, and the value of perseverance. They instilled in me the values of protecting my family and helping others in need. I thought of them as I always do as I wrote this book. When times get tough, keep pushing through. Creating this book is a great accomplishment, and I hope I made them proud.

ACKNOWLEDGMENTS

I want to express my gratitude to Erica Bravo for her invaluable assistance and guidance in designing my tracking sheets. A special thank you to Katrina Watters for editing, formatting, and providing valuable advice throughout the process. To Michelle Rangel, my fellow behavioral therapist and work bestie, who always comes in the clutch and provides me with professional advice. To my family and friends who provided guidance and advice in countless ways, thank you for your love and support.

CONTENTS

WELCOME TO ABA: BEHAVIOR BASICS

This book will serve as a guide to the fundamentals of applied behavior analysis (ABA). According to Virginia Commonwealth University's Autism Center for Education, "The ultimate goal of ABA is to establish and enhance socially important behaviors. Such behaviors can include academic, social, communication, and daily living skills; essentially, any skill that will enhance the independence and/or quality of life for the individual."

As a behavioral therapist with years of ABA experience, I've had the privilege of witnessing the transformation of many children's behaviors. I have worked with individuals ranging from three to twenty-six years old. My grandmother always said, "Get me once, shame on you; get me twice, shame on me." I have used this throughout my time as a behavioral therapist. I always pay attention to a child's maladaptive behavior to adjust my response so the child doesn't exhibit it again. In life, we will encounter a myriad of behaviors, both good and bad. Regardless of the behavior, understanding and knowing how to effectively manage it is essential.

I will introduce ways to pay attention to your child's behavior. I wrote this book because I have a passion for helping people. I created tracking sheets to help you in your journey of understanding your child's behavior. I'm a behavioral therapist, so I know these strategies work because I use them every single day. They don't work the same in every scenario because every child is different, but they work. The title of this book is *The Behavior Toolbox* because behavioral therapists must have many tools in their toolboxes to navigate the day when working with children with different behaviors. I want to equip caregivers with as many tools as I can so they have a clearer understanding of how to respond to behaviors.

This book provides insight into understanding, shaping, and modifying behavior. I will give you strategies and tools to help you manage and understand your child's behavior. You will learn how to reinforce positive behavior, address challenging behavior, and create an environment that promotes your child's growth.

Has your child ever not responded when you greet them? There's a strategy for that! If the child doesn't respond to your greeting, prompt them by saying, "No, try again. Hi, (child's name)." I will provide more examples as you read through this book.

You'll discover empowering techniques to enhance communication and build a foundation for a lasting positive change in your child's life. By understanding the basics of ABA, you can gain valuable tools and strategies to help foster meaningful connections. Honing your ability to interpret, respond, and recognize behaviors effectively will foster a greater understanding of your child.

Central to the exploration of behavior is regulation and the ability to control one's emotions and thoughts in response to internal and external stimuli. Dysregulation can lead to challenges and maladaptive behaviors. I will teach you strategies to help your child handle feeling dysregulated. Whether you are a parent, caregiver, or just someone trying to understand human behavior, this book will provide a roadmap to comprehensive strategies that will help you unlock the mysteries of behavior. Welcome to a transformative exploration of strategies for handling behaviors. May this journey be both enriching and enlightening.

CHAPTER 1

NAVIGATING AGGRESSION: A STRATEGIC APPROACH

This chapter explores aggressive behavior and provides actionable strategies for parents and caregivers to handle it in a supportive manner. Aggression can be challenging to address, so we will approach it from a preventative lens. Aggression is complex and manifests in forms such as verbal, physical, and relational aggression. You need to understand the root cause to implement an effective strategy.

Types of Aggression

Physical Aggression is defined as physically harming oneself, other people, or objects. This can include hitting, kicking, punching, or damaging property.

Verbal Aggression is using words to hurt other people, such as threats, yelling, or insults.

Relational Aggression is a form of behavior intended to harm someone's relationships, social status, or self-esteem within a group—a non-physical form of bullying.

Understanding the function of aggression helps tailor interventions to address and replace it with adaptive behaviors. In ABA, aggressive behavior in children is understood through a lens of functional analysis, which seeks to find the function or cause of the behavior. Identifying the function of aggression through the outburst tracker is crucial. You can use the tracking sheets to help start implementing interventions that will help you manage the behaviors.

Prevention is key in managing aggression. I suggest these preventative measures:

- **Teach emotional regulation skills:** Talk to your child about their feelings and how to label them; teach healthy ways to express them. Encourage deep breathing, counting to ten, or taking a break when feeling frustrated.
- **Promote positive reinforcement:** Acknowledge and praise appropriate behavior, such as turn-taking, sharing, or using words to express themselves.
- **Encourage effective communication:** Teach the child to express needs verbally rather than through aggression. Model respectful communication in your interactions.
- **Provide opportunities for physical play:** Regular physical activity helps release pent-up energy and reduce stress. Recreational activities can help channel aggression in a positive direction.
- **Create a safe and nurturing environment:** Make sure the child feels safe, supported, and loved.
- **Teach problem-solving skills:** Most aggression comes from rigidity and/or the inability to compromise. Teach the child how to negotiate, compromise, or seek help from an adult if needed.

In addition to the challenges of aggressive behavior toward others, children often engage in self-harming behaviors. These can manifest in ways that require special attention and lots of understanding. Trying to unravel the complexities of self-harm in children takes time and patience.

If your child engages in self-harm, consider the following: Everyday sights and sounds can cause sensory overload and overwhelm a child's ability to regulate and process information. Experiences that most people take for granted can overwhelm children who are extremely sensitive, such as textures of clothing against skin, lights, and crowded rooms. Sensory overload may lead to self-harm in an attempt to regain control and find relief. Sensory experiences can play a role in self-harm as children use the sensation as a distraction from emotional pain or to feel a sense of control in chaos. I have discovered calming sensory strips can assist children in managing sensory overload. You can place different sizes of these strips around the house for whenever your child needs them.

For some children, self-harm is a way to regulate overwhelming emotions by creating physical pain; it temporarily overrides emotional distress. The sensory experience of pain offers a tangible outlet for emotional pain while providing a temporary sense of release. While it may provide relief, it doesn't address the problem or underlying issues causing distress. With all behavior, it's important to seek an understanding of its function and address it accordingly.

Communication difficulties present unique challenges for children expressing thoughts, needs, and emotions and sometimes lead to self-harm. For children who struggle to communicate verbally or interpret social cues, self-harm can become a means of expressing distress, frustration, or displeasure with a situation. When other methods of communication have failed to convey their inner turmoil, they may turn to self-harm to communicate discomfort or pain.

The child's inability to effectively communicate emotions or seek help exacerbates feelings of isolation. Without the skillset to articulate their emotional state or the social awareness to understand others, some children turn to self-harm to cope with anxiety and sadness. Additionally, communication difficulties can hinder the caregiver's ability to recognize and respond to the child's needs because of misinterpreting self-harm as attention-seeking or defiance, leading to inadequate support and intervention. It is crucial for parents to recognize the communication function of self-harm and approach it with understanding, empathy, and a commitment to support effective communication. By addressing miscommunication barriers, you reduce the likelihood of self-harm behaviors.

Rituals are common in children; they seek solace in repetitive behaviors and rituals to regain control and security. However, when rituals become rigid and all-consuming, they can escalate into self-harm.

Anxiety can be debilitating for children; it colors thoughts, perceptions, and actions in shades of apprehension and fear. From everyday routines to social interactions, anxiety can permeate every aspect of life, exacerbating stress and triggering self-harm as a maladaptive coping mechanism.

While rituals and anxiety pose significant challenges, there are strategies to reduce the risk of self-harm. These strategies can help your child cultivate healthier coping mechanisms and enhance their overall well-being.

- **Establish a predictable routine:** Consistency and predictability reduce anxiety by providing structure (e.g., daily schedule, regular bedtime routine, and consistent mealtimes).
- **Teach relaxation techniques:** Relaxation techniques, such as mindful meditation, deep breathing exercises, and muscle relaxation, can calm the mind and body.
- **Provide sensory accommodations:** Provide a rest break in a sensory-friendly area with noise-canceling headphones, a weighted blanket, and fidgets.
- **Offer visual support:** Use visuals like social stories and visual timers to help the child understand and anticipate transitions.
- **Encourage verbal expression:** Encourage the child to express and verbalize feelings, thoughts, and concerns rather than relying on ritualistic behaviors as your means of communication.

- **Develop flexible thinking:** Develop problem-solving and flexibility skills by teaching alternative ways to approach situations, cope with change, and reduce reliance on rituals.
- **Offer social support:** Encourage your child to build social connections by engaging in social activities or joining peer groups. Participate in social skills programs to reduce feelings of isolation and anxiety.
- **Model healthy coping behaviors:** Model healthy coping behaviors and emotions you want your child to see. Demonstrating positive strategies to manage stress and anxiety will show your child they are capable of doing the same.
- **Seek professional guidance:** Consult your healthcare provider if you have exhausted all resources and are still not able to manage the behaviors.

An effective strategy is switching out individuals who may trigger challenging behavior. Switching out is a crucial aspect of effective behavior management and support; it's essential to recognize certain people may inadvertently contribute to the child's behavior escalation or cause distress due to their interactions or communication style. If you notice your child reacts negatively or exhibits challenging behavior in the presence of a particular person, address the dynamic to prevent further escalation and promote a positive environment.

Switching out individuals also allows a new perspective on a situation and a break in potentially escalating interactions. Children respond differently to individuals based on their relationships and communication styles. If the child is mad at a particular person, a new person may have more success calming and de-escalating the situation. Rotating caregivers provides opportunities for new and different approaches that may be more conducive to the child's well-being and behavior management.

Changing caregivers will help with burnout, so one person is not always handling the behavior and provides a much-needed break. Continuously being the one handling behavior can lead to stress and frustration for caregivers. Implementing a system where caregivers switch and rotate fosters a supportive and sustainable home environment where everyone feels they work as a team for the child's betterment.

There are several effective strategies to approach and address aggressive behavior. If a child shows early signs of aggression, remove the stimulus (whether a person or object, like a game). This allows for a break, and returning later can help with managing emotions. Pay attention to signs that alert you to aggression, such as grunting noises or repeatedly making oppositional statements to a request. Once aggression escalates, I've found giving hand and arm massages can be calming if the child feels enough pressure. Though it may require initially taking a few hits, getting close enough to massage the hands aids relaxation. Reflexology may introduce techniques that work for your child because some children like foot massages. As you get closer, let your child know you are going to give hand, arm, or leg massages so they understand what you are going to do. Try the massage for a minute or two. If it seems like it's not working, try another strategy, such as a weighted blanket. Another way to provide pressure is using a blocking pad or some other firm item you have nearby; the child can safely push against, punch, or kick it. Finally, strive to contain the space to minimize damage and maximize safety by closing the door.

Ultimately, your response to aggression depends on your child. By implementing the strategies that work for you, you can better manage behavior and foster a supportive, nurturing environment that provides growth.

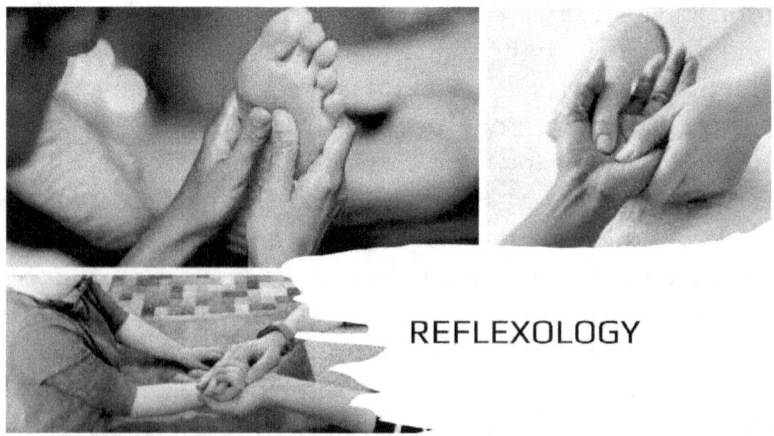

REFLEXOLOGY

Strategies for Approaching Aggressive Behavior

Remain calm.

- Stay composed when faced with aggression; responding with anger or aggression may escalate the situation.

Assess the situation.

- Is the child or the caregiver in immediate danger? Do you need to evacuate the area? Assess your capabilities, if you need assistance, and how soon you should call for assistance.

Remove potentially dangerous objects.

- Look around the area for anything that could be used as a weapon and remove it or put it out of reach.

Set boundaries.

- Clearly communicate the consequences of aggression; plan to follow through with enforcing them.

Listen actively.

- Listen to the child and validate their feelings and concerns.

Provide support.

- Teach coping skills like relaxation techniques and provide assistance in managing emotions with counseling services.

Teach conflict resolution.

- Help develop healthy ways to resolve conflicts without resulting in aggression by using compromise, communication, and negotiating.

Implement behavioral interventions.

- These techniques can be positive or negative to encourage or discourage behaviors. Positive reinforcements like token economies encourage positive behavior; implement a time-out procedure to discourage aggression.

Promote a positive environment.

- Encourage positive interactions and provide an environment that fosters empathy, respect, and cooperation.

Practice self-care.

- Caregivers who are supporting aggressive individuals can be emotionally drained. You must maintain your well-being and prioritize self-care before you can help someone else.

Properly managing aggressive behavior requires understanding the underlying cause and responding with appropriate strategies. Once you discern the cause, start implementing preventative strategies. I will provide several tracking sheets at the end of the book so you can keep behavior data. An example of a tracking sheet is on the next page.

OUTBURST TRACKER

Date:	Start Time:	Finish Time:

Duration::	Location:

Triggers:

What went well:

What actions were taken:

What Happened:

Strategies used:

Figure 1: Example of tracking sheet

CHAPTER 2

DECODING BEHAVIORS

This chapter will dive into the intricacies of understanding, shaping, and modifying behaviors. I will define behavior and give its functions. This chapter also provides tools to decode behavior and implement effective interventions. Behaviors may be verbal, nonverbal, conscious, or unconscious. Children exhibit different behaviors in different situations for different reasons.

Behavior has four functions: *attention, escape/avoidance, access to tangibles,* and *automatic reinforcement.*

Attention

Seeking attention from adults or peers by using disruptive behaviors such as loud talking, interrupting conversations, and making noise. Respond with planned ignoring, which is withholding attention to the unwanted behavior. When the child displays desirable behavior, parents respond with positive attention.

Escape/Avoidance

Escaping or avoiding an unpleasant task occurs when an unpleasant request is made. It looks like a refusal to work, stalling, and avoiding the area altogether. A student may be disruptive in class to avoid an assignment. Modify the workload and give the child breaks and choices of when to complete the task.

Access to Tangible

Trying to obtain access to a desired object or activity. A toy, food, or electronic device is so rewarding the child will do anything to gain access to it. Encourage the use of words to gain access to the object instead of maladaptive behavior (like tantrums). If the child is nonverbal, use the Picture Exchange System (PECS) or Augmentative and Alternative Communication device (AAC). I will talk about these later in the book.

Automatic Reinforcement

Repetitive behaviors like hand-flapping and rocking are sensory-seeking behaviors. They produce sensory comfort for the child; it may be hard to redirect these behaviors because they are self-soothing and provide comfort. Use strategies that contradict the behavior, such as giving a fidget to hold instead of hand flapping if you find the behavior is inappropriate for the setting.

When a behavioral therapist talks about the ABCs, this refers to Antecedents, Behavior, and Consequences.

- **Antecedent:** what happened before the behavior and what was going on immediately before the child's behavior.
- **Behavior:** anything observable and measurable or an individual's actions.
- **Consequence:** reinforcing or punitive response depending on whether the goal is to increase or decrease the behavior.

The antecedent sets the stage for behavior; it includes environmental cues, social interactions, verbal instructions, and internal thoughts. Understanding the antecedent provides valuable information about what influenced the behavior and helps identify the trigger. This is true for both desirable and maladaptive behaviors. Developing a modification strategy for antecedents may decrease the likelihood of a repeat of behavior. For example, the child exhibits maladaptive behavior whenever it's time to clean up. Modify the antecedent (the phrase "clean up") by instead saying, "I'll help you put your things away, and you move one item."

Understanding behavior is the focal point of tracking. I made the tracking sheets to allow you to track the frequency, duration, and characteristics of behaviors. You are trained observers and don't even know it; you see and deal with behavior every day. You can now collect and track the data with these sheets.

Consequences strengthen or weaken the likelihood of repeated behavior depending on reinforcement or punishment. Reinforcement serves as a powerful tool by providing rewards for positive behavior. For example, present a reward when you see positive behavior so your child connects desired items with desired behavior.

Finding the ABCs reveals patterns of underlying functions of behavior. What happens before the behavior is key to figuring out what triggers your child. *Trigger* is another way to say *antecedent*. It may be as seemingly simple as a loud noise or a schedule change. As parents, these things seem simple to us, but they are not simple to the child. I believe a big part of parent training is shedding our thoughts and trying to take the child's perspective. You can't always give in, but having a little empathy goes a long way. If you can identify the trigger, it will help you understand the function of your child's behavior.

CHAPTER 3

EXPLORING TRIGGERS

This chapter looks at triggers and explores how they shape our responses. Triggers are stimuli that prompt a particular response or reaction, essentially what causes maladaptive behavior. Triggers play a vital role in guiding our thoughts and behaviors. We will seek to unravel the complexities of triggers' impact on daily life.

Learning a child's triggers prepares you by increasing your ability to head them off and prevent resulting behavior altogether. Tracking triggers is critical because there are several strategies you can employ once you understand them.

Common Triggers

- Loud noises
- Bright lights
- Strong smells
- Crowded environment
- Hunger

- Lack of sleep
- Physical illness
- Academics
- Transitioning between activities
- Temperature
- Clothing texture
- Cognitive overload
- Peer conflict

Parents often overlook the medication trigger. Medication can affect behavior in both positive and negative ways. Many medications have side effects that may impact behavior. It is crucial to track dosage changes and resulting side effects, including mood swings, agitation, or irritability. This helps your healthcare providers adjust your child's medications. If you find medication is a trigger, work with your healthcare provider to find the right dosage. The tracker may reveal changes in behavior in correlation with the doses. Overall, medications can be valuable in managing maladaptive behavior once you find the right dosage. Use the sheet provided to begin tracking medication changes.

medication tracker.

medication	dose	start	stop	side effects

Figure 2: Example of medication tracker

Noise and light can also be triggers. Noises like fire alarms or playgrounds are common triggers at school. Your child may be overwhelmed by loud sounds and try to elope. Work with school staff and let the child know of a pending fire alarm so they have noise-canceling headphones accessible and can be away from bells when they sound. If your child is overwhelmed by playground noise, you can work with the teacher and try an alternative recess. The child still gets to play but in a different area.

Children with light sensitivity may benefit from transition glasses that help when entering different rooms. You can buy light coverings to dim lights in a room. Pack a bag with headphones, earplugs, and sunglasses, and leave them in the car so you always have them in case you need them.

Schedules can be a trigger, leading to outbursts. Making a visual schedule will help your child know what to expect daily. You can make a picture schedule or write it down. Here are a few steps to follow when organizing a schedule system:

- Decide where to put the schedule. Make sure it is easily accessible.
- Make a display board with Velcro to change events and activities easily.
- Make the pictures big enough to see.
- Refer to the schedule throughout the day and use it to let the child know what to expect next.
- Make sure all caregivers are aware of the schedule, and they know where it is posted.

When there is a schedule change, inform the child beforehand. This is called *priming*. The picture schedule below is an effective example to incorporate into your child's daily life. You can make the schedule yourself.

Figure 3: Example of a daily schedule board

- **Make a schedule board:** I suggest using Canva (they have free templates) and laminating the board.
- **Figure out activities:** Find activity icons you want to include on the schedule from the internet. This could be the daily routine, special event, or preferred activity pictures—for example, a picture of a book for reading time or bed for bedtime.
- **Print:** Print, laminate, and cut out the pictures.
- **Gather materials:** Add Velcro circles to the schedule board and the back of the picture cards.
- **Add any extra details:** Add anything specific you would like, such as times, special instructions, or special activities.
- **Hang your board:** Once everything is arranged, put the board in a place where it is easily accessible and use it daily.
- **Update regularly:** Keep the activities current and update the board when necessary.

CHAPTER 4

THE POWER OF PRIMING AND MODIFYING

Priming should be considered the first line of defense against maladaptive behavior. Priming sets your child up for success by preparing them for what is about to happen. For instance, if you know there will be a substitute instead of the teacher tomorrow, let your child know so they can process the information. Priming's goal is to prepare the child so they know what to expect, which in turn lessens maladaptive behavior. Some children find comfort in routine and are rigid if the schedule is changed without notice. Another way to prime your child is by saying, "The iPad will turn off in two minutes." This indicates that their time is about to end, so they are not surprised when the iPad turns off.

If priming doesn't work, you can modify the request or task. Modifying the task means breaking it into smaller, more manageable steps. The child can focus on one step instead of the entire task. This makes things less frustrating. Simplifying and breaking down instructions helps a child's understanding. For instance, if writing is a non-preferred task, offer to scribe while they tell you what to write. The work is completed with a bit of modification.

When discerning where modification is needed, you must identify the task requiring assistance and consider where you can maximize success and promote skill development. For example, if the content of a worksheet is too large, try completing the odd-number problems on the first day. The child can tackle the even-number problems the following day. Giving your child a choice between options allows them to feel they have input and a sense of control.

Parents, you can also change the wording of a request. Most children dislike the phrase "clean up." Change it to, "Let's put these things away" or, "I can help you pick up your things," and push the toys toward the child.

Demonstrate the task's steps and ask the child to observe what you do. Modeling helps children understand expectations. Prompting and fading, such as verbal cues, gestures, and physical guidance, may be used to provide support and guidance. Slowly fade out prompts as the child becomes more independent.

The first/then strategy is another effective technique. Start by completing a less preferred task, then offer a more preferred task. Identify the task, determine what needs to be done, and then figure out the sequence. For instance, homework must be completed *first*, and _then_ we can play a video game. Offer choices whenever possible; the child can choose whether they want to read or do math homework before they get the video game. Kids love to voice their opinions, so give choices whenever possible.

Steps to make a first/then board:

- Prepare a board. You can find free templates on Canva.
- Draw the first/then sections and laminate the page.
- Attach Velcro dots.
- Select pictures or symbols you want to use. Print, laminate, and Velcro them.
- Update as needed.

FIRST/THEN BOARD

First   **Then**

PRIMING STRATEGIES	
Establish a routine	Use visual supports
Use timers	Break tasks into smaller steps
Relaxation techniques	Calm and self-regulation techniques
Social stories	Choices
Positive reinforcement	Muscle relaxation
Environmental modifications	Breathing exercises
Praise	Sensory accommodations
First/then strategies	Provide supportive guidance
Offer breaks	Be consistent
Model expected behavior	Usc positive language to frame the task
Make it fun	clear expectations

Figure 5: Priming strategies examples

Prevention is of paramount importance. After observing your child and identifying triggers and the function of behavior, you can start to implement prevention strategies. Utilizing and monitoring the strategies' efficacy will greatly assist you on your journey to preventing maladaptive behavior. Below is a monthly tracker featuring various strategies crafted to assist with this goal. Simply check off the strategy you've tried and note the result. Feel free to add any necessary notes. Using multiple strategies simultaneously may be the most effective approach. For example, providing a snack break with a timer, informing the child when their time is nearly up, and communicating upcoming activities on the schedule.

STRATEGY TRACKER   MONTH:

Habit	1	2	3	4	5	6	7	8	9	10	11	12	13	14	15	16	17	18	19	20	21	22	23	24	25	26	27	28	29	30	31	Result
Use Timers																																
Visual Supports																																
Snacks (eating)																																
First/Then Board																																
Offer Breaks																																
Choices																																
Sensory accommodations																																
Breathing Exercises																																
Environmental Modifications																																
Priming																																
Break Task Into Smaller Steps																																
Notes:																																

CHAPTER 5

FINDING BALANCE:
CALM AMIDST THE STORM

We employ various strategies in ABA to help regulate children's emotions. Some parents may feel their child is a "little off" or "not their usual self." This is *dysregulation*, a disruption in behavioral equilibrium that leads to unwanted, maladaptive behaviors. It may manifest in several ways, such as impulsivity, difficulty managing emotions, and anxiety. Behavior can range from an angry outburst to self-harm. Children may have mood swings and irritability that impact them daily. Every child is different, so you will observe dysregulation showing up uniquely in your child. Utilizing calming strategies may help you regain control, manage dysregulation more effectively, and enhance your child's overall health. Here are a few ways to teach skills that help regulate emotions and behavior while creating a supportive environment:

- **Establish routines:** Regular mealtimes, bedtimes, and a daily schedule will provide structure and consistency.

- **Teach emotional awareness:** Work with your child to help them figure out their emotions and discuss those emotions with them. Teach them it is okay to express emotions and validate their feelings.
- **Practice mindfulness:** Teach calming techniques like deep-breathing exercises, coloring, and meditation to help them become aware of their thoughts.
- **Encourage self-regulation:** Teach calming strategies like counting to ten and positive self-talk.
- **Provide a safe space:** Create a space in your home where the child can go to calm down when dysregulated. You may call it the "calm corner" or "cozy corner." Include pillows, a weighted blanket, and preferred items.
- **Model healthy coping skills:** You are a role model for desired behavior by managing your emotions in a healthy way. Demonstrate problem-solving skills and empathy in your life.
- **Positive reinforcement:** Reward the child when you notice positive behavior. Praise the child for using self-regulating skills.
- **Limit screen time:** Too much screen time can disrupt sleep patterns and contribute to dysregulation. Establish a time limit and encourage other activities.
- **Seek professional help:** If your child still struggles with dysregulation despite trying all these strategies, seek guidance from your pediatrician or therapist. They can provide personalized strategies of support.

Every child responds differently to strategies, so it may be challenging to find what works best. Don't get discouraged!

Creating a sensory calming corner provides a safe, soothing place for the child to regulate emotions. You can work together to choose a space for retreat when they need a break or feel overwhelmed. Decorate it with sensory-friendly materials like a bean bag, weighted blanket, and pillows. Add sensory tools like fidgets, stress balls, music, or textured items like a small sandbox. Some children like coloring books or reading books for relaxation. Create visual cues like break cards that signal the need for a calming break and do regular check-ins to see if breaks are needed. An example of a check-in would be saying, "Hey, little buddy, would you like a three-minute break or a five-minute break?" Show the cards and have the child pick one. The following page has examples of break cards and what typically goes in a calming corner. I've found that five-minute breaks work best. If your child needs more time, try adding one minute and go from there.

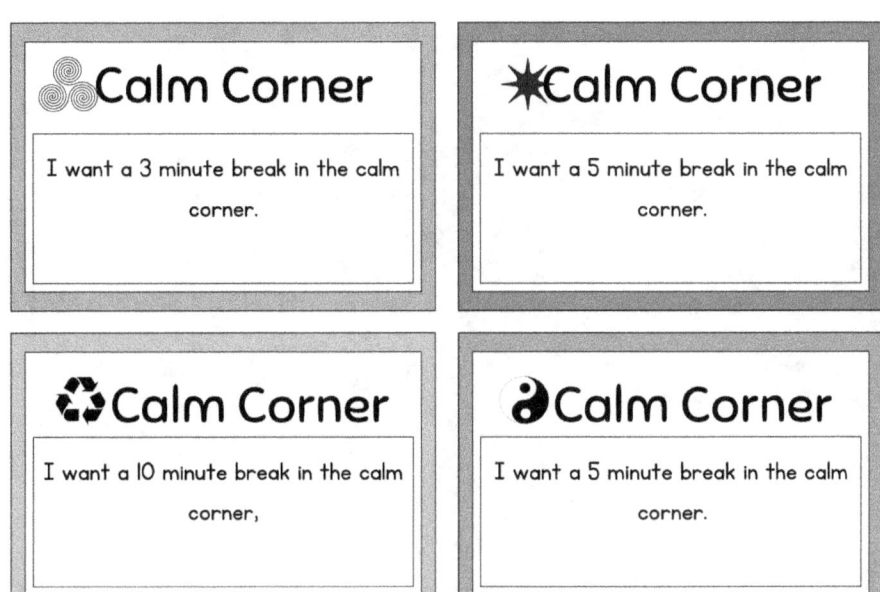

Next, we will explore a wide range of strategies designed to enhance and foster emotional regulation. As I mentioned in Chapter 3, you will often observe a sign or a signal that a maladaptive behavior is coming; you can employ a calming strategy In these moments to prevent it.

Intervention use is based on the functions of behaviors. Functional communication training teaches the child acceptable ways to communicate needs. This sounds like telling the child to use their words to get what they want and practicing the skill. This helps reduce reliance on maladaptive behavior. Antecedent interventions modify the environment to reduce triggers, like providing visuals and prompting before you see a maladaptive behavior. Do a functional behavior assessment when you finish tracking, gathering all the information to determine the behavior's function.

It is essential to try different strategies to find which work and which will trigger your child and make the situation worse. If feasible, ask your child which strategies they would like to try. Always remember that *just because a strategy worked in the past doesn't mean it will always work*, so be prepared with another strategy. You must always have another tool in your toolbox when a strategy doesn't work; make sure you are prepared with a backup plan. If your child has outbursts outside of home, pack a backpack and keep it in the car at the ready. Include fidgets, coloring books, bubbles, snacks, water, and little toys in an emergency behavior bag.

When implementing these approaches, remember that each child is unique and that some techniques may work better than others. That's why tracking strategies is important to see patterns of efficacy. Additionally, ongoing tracking, communication, and collaboration with your healthcare providers are essential.

CALMING STRATEGIES	
Weighted blankets	Create a calm corner
Fidgets	Music
Blow bubbles	Take a break (have a snack, read, be alone)
Yell into a pillow	Rip paper or boxes
Break popsicle sticks	Go for a walk
Pressure massage (head, arms, legs)	Headphones, earplugs
Give space (set a timer and check in)	Drawing
Deep breathing	Drink water
Make a fort	Squeeze playdough or clay
Chewing gum	Kinetic sand
Play with slime	Run a lap
Legos	Stress ball

Figure 6: Examples of calming strategies

CHAPTER 6

SHAPING BEHAVIORS:
THE POWER OF REINFORCEMENTS

Reinforcements are vital to shaping behavior, actions, and decisions. Reinforcements can be as simple as verbal praise or as intricate as a reward store system. We will go through different rewards to find the best ones for your child. Conduct a preference assessment to determine what your child likes and is motivated by. Avoid randomly selecting reinforcements and rewards; this approach may not effectively reduce maladaptive behavior.

You can decide if *intermittent* or *schedule*d reinforcement is most effective. Intermittent means randomly catching expected behavior and offering a reward. Scheduled means a reinforcement is given every time for the desired behavior. Scheduled or intermittent reinforcements may lead to stronger and more persistent behavior if the child associates the reward with the expected behavior. The reward must be motivating to be effective.

The token system is currency to reinforce desired behavior. Tokens can be objects like coins, points, stars, stickers, and fake money. They serve as a tangible reward for and representation of expected behavior. Together, you will determine specific behaviors that earn tokens. These could be following instructions, doing chores, or any other desired behavior. A token is earned each time the child exhibits the predetermined behavior. Once the child has accumulated a certain number of tokens, they can be exchanged for a predetermined reward—as small as a toy from the dollar store or as large as a new bike. You must be consistent with reinforcements and reward with tokens when you see the desired behavior. Keep track of your child's earned tokens. It helps if you keep the tracker in a place where everyone can see the progress. When you see your child showing mastery, increase the difficulty level of earning tokens by changing the desired behaviors.

A reward store system reinforces desired behaviors through the exchange of points, tokens, stars, or money. Implement these steps before setting up your store.

1. Tell your child what the expected tasks or behaviors are.
2. Establish the token economy you will use.

    -   Will you be using points, coins, stars, or fake money? Will they be physical or digital?
    -   Where will you keep track of the points earned? Will it be a physical or digital tracker?
    -   Selecting reinforcement items for the store should be motivating.
    -   Set prices for items; make sure prices are reasonable and achievable.

3. Establish rules for the store, such as when items can be purchased.

    -   Rules should include guidelines for behavior expectations, token distribution, and consequences for rule violations.
    -   Be consistent with the upkeep of the store and the items.

4. Track the effectiveness of the reward store system; make necessary adjustments.
5. Provide feedback to your child.

- Praise positive behavior and award extra points or tokens for exceptional behavior. This is usually very motivating to a child and promotes positive behavior change.

You can implement a token board system. A token board is a visual tool used in behavioral management. It is usually a board with five spaces for tokens with tasks listed for the child to complete. As the child completes the task, they receive a token on the board. Once a certain number of tokens are earned, they earn a reward or reinforcement. Token boards are effective in providing structure, motivation, and reinforcement to achieve goals. The following provides step-by-step instructions for making a token board.

- **Gather materials:** You will need to make a template on Canva or PowerPoint to create the board and tokens.
- **Design the board:** Decide how you want the board to look. Do you want designs or pictures on the border? Add a title to the board.
- **Divide the board into sections:** Decide how many sections you want on the board. It is most common to have five or ten. Each section represents a task to be completed.
- **Add reward cards:** What is the child working toward by completing the tasks? Laminate all materials that were made.
- **Attach Velcro dots:** Attach Velcro dots to the board and the backs of the tokens. Make sure there is enough space between each dot to easily attach and remove.

By following these steps, you can create a customized token board to help motivate and reinforce desired behavior.

Here is an example of a completed token board featuring tokens and reinforcement pieces.

Token Board

Once your token board is complete, proceed with the following steps:

- **Introduce the token board:** Explain the token system to the child and let them know each time they complete a task or demonstrate positive behavior, they earn a token to be placed on the board.

- **Reward system:** Determine the number of tokens needed to earn the reward. It can be a small reward, screen time, or a preferred activity.

- **Celebrate success:** Once the child has earned all the tokens, celebrate their success and provide the reward.

- **Review and adjust:** Regularly review if the token board is working and adjust the tasks, rewards, or the layout of the board as necessary to better suit the child.

CHAPTER 7

STRENGTHENING BONDS THROUGH PROCESSING

After any storm of emotions subsides, process what happened with your child and provide support and guidance. This crucial phase allows the child to reflect, process, and restore a relationship if needed. They need to understand the consequences of their actions and learn ways of coping with difficult situations.

Processing provides the opportunity to understand and identify emotions that led to the outburst. Discussing feelings in a safe environment helps recognize the signs of anger, frustration, or sadness before they escalate into outbursts. This understanding empowers the child to express emotions in a healthier way and ask for help when needed.

Processing together helps build self-awareness by reflecting on the behavior and its impact on others. Expressing thoughts and feelings verbally with parents helps build positive communication and foster healthy dialogue. Processing fosters a healthier emotional relationship and promotes personal growth. Explain processing as self-reflection and acknowledgment of wrongdoing and discuss the importance of understanding the impact of their actions on other people. Emphasize the importance of apologizing, demonstrating accountability, and desiring to repair impacted relationships.

Sometimes, it is hard for children to express themselves; in this case, draw pictures of what happened or write an apology and give it to the affected person. You can make custom apology sheets in Canva; these should reflect your child's age and capabilities. I have an example of what an apology sheet can look like. It was created in Canva, and what you want the template to say is customizable.

You want to help your child understand their emotions, learn from the experience, and develop strategies to help manage situations in the future. Processing involves several components:

Provide a safe space.

- Create a calm and supportive environment for processing. Find a comfortable and distraction-free area that allows for focus.

Acknowledge the outburst.

- Guide your child to accept that the outburst happened and say what they did, accepting responsibility for their actions.

Identify the triggers and emotions.

- Reflect on what led up to the outburst and what the feelings were. Understanding the emotion(s) can prevent a future recurrence.

Identify healthy coping strategies.

- Talk about strategies to use next time the situation arises.

Apologize and make amends.

- If the outburst affects other people, the child should make a sincere apology, take responsibility for their actions, and show genuine intention in rebuilding the relationship.

Cultivate resilience.

- View the outburst as an opportunity for growth and learn from the experience. Resilience allows you to bounce back from setbacks and better handle future challenges.

Remember, healing is a process. Each phase will bring you closer to your child and help their emotional well-being. Processing after an outburst is a journey to self-discovery. We must emphasize self-awareness, accountability, and personal growth after an outburst.

The sheet below will help provide insight into how your child felt before and after the outburst. Fill out a sheet for every outburst and review the results with your healthcare provider.

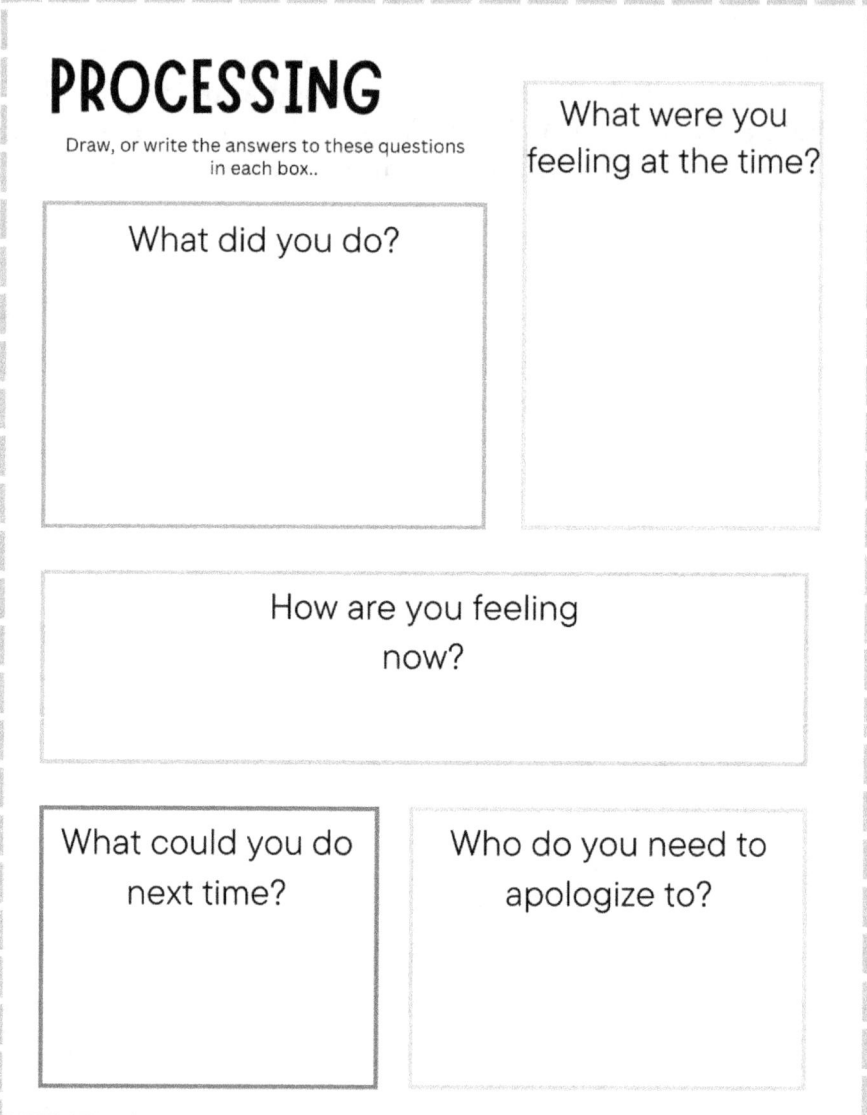

Figure 7: Processing tracking sheet

CHAPTER 8

FOUNDATIONS OF EFFECTIVE COMMUNICATIONS

Communication is fundamental and unique to everyone. We will explore different forms of communication in ABA. Communication can be a difficult challenge. I will teach you more about three supportive communication strategies that may help your child feel more independent and supported. They are the *picture exchange system* (PECS), *augmentative and alternative communication* (AAC), and *sign language*. All three are beneficial forms of communication. I recommend you pick one and use it exclusively until it's mastered; then, you can move on to another if preferred.

Picture Exchange System (PECS)

PECS is a simple yet effective approach to using pictures and symbols to facilitate communication between individuals. In PECS, the child uses pictures or symbols to communicate needs. The child is taught to exchange a picture card representing a desired item with the teacher or caregiver. PECS is individually tailored and designed to enhance communication while reducing maladaptive behavior. Children learn to communicate independently through visual support and systematic prompting, promoting autonomy and reducing frustration. PECS empowers children to participate fully in their environment. You can make a PECS binder:

- **Select the materials:** Gather a binder, page protectors, Velcro strips, and communication pictures. The pictures should be relevant to your child's needs.
- **Set up the binder:** Break it up into sections such as food, people, places, and activities. Use dividers or tabs to separate the sections so the child can navigate through the book.
- **Prepare the pages:** Arrange the pictures on each page in an organized manner so the child can clearly see each picture. Ensure each picture has enough space on each page and is clearly labeled.
- **Attach the Velcro:** Attach Velcro strips to the back of each picture and place them on each page to make sure they are easily attached and removed.
- **Implement the system:** Introduce the binder to the child and all caregivers. Teach the child to request items by handing you a picture in exchange for the item. Encourage regular practice using PECS to promote independence.
- **Update and maintain:** Review the book for maintenance and upkeep periodically to ensure the pictures are still clearly visible and reflect your child's preferences and needs.

Following these steps will create a functional and personalized PECS binder to support your child's communication and language development.

FINISHED PECS BOARD

Figure 8: Picture of how the finished PECS book should look.

Augmentative and Alternative Communication (AAC)

The AAC device comes in various forms, such as a tablet with apps or a speech-generating device. It operates by supplementing or replacing speech and giving the child a communication alternative. The AAC device is individually programmed. It is the voice of the child; the child puts in a request, and the device reads what the child requested. There are many apps that can be installed on your iPad to help your child communicate in this way. A therapist should support the family with inputting pictures, making sentences, and navigating the device.

The goals of an AAC are independence and a better quality of life. The benefit of the device extends beyond facilitating communication; it helps promote social interaction, participation, and independence. The AAC device empowers the child to express preferences and make choices in different settings. As technology advances, the devices become increasingly customizable, portable, and user-friendly. Below are a few of the current speech apps you can install on a tablet or iPad.

- Proloquo2Go
- Proloquo
- Sonoflex
- Speech Assistant
- TouchChat HD
- MyTalkTools Mobile Pro
- Avaz
- ICOMM
- QuickTalk AAC
- Visuals2Go
- Lamp Words for Life
- TalkTablet PRO Autism, Aphasia

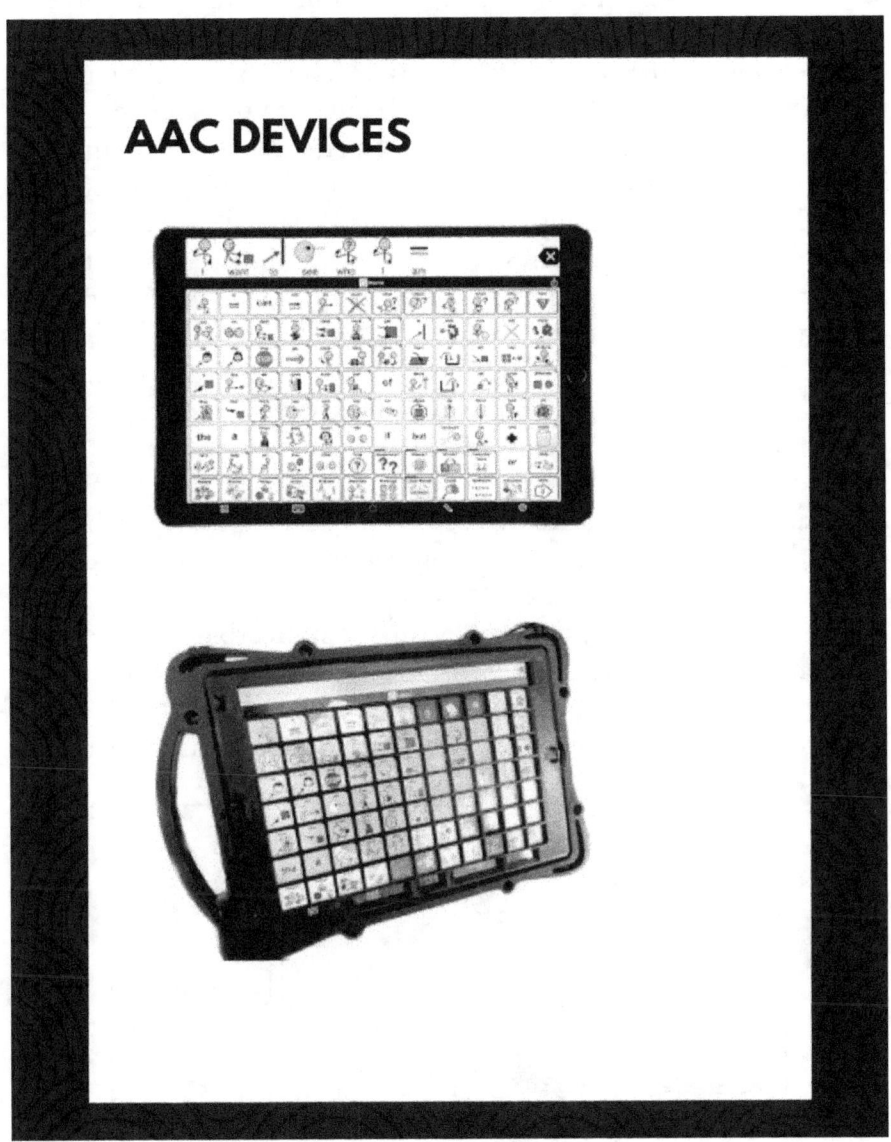

Figure 9: Samples of AAC devices

Sign Language

Sign language is a complex system of communication that utilizes visual-manual gestures, facial expressions, and body movements. Unlike spoken language, which relies on sound, sign language primarily relies on visuals. Sign language enables the user to express a wide range of emotions and concepts. American Sign Language (ASL) is the most widely recognized. ASL consists of movements, handshapes, and locations to represent words and concepts. Facial expressions and body postures all contribute to the meanings of signs.

Sign language has numerous benefits for nonverbal individuals. Signing provides an alternative means of communication and allows self-expression. It is challenging when a child wants something and is unable to communicate their needs. Sign language allows children and parents to communicate with each other and other people across various settings and situations. As awareness of sign language grows, efforts to promote accessibility continue to expand. See the chart on the following page for some of the most common signs people learn in ABA.

Using sign language is powerful for nonverbal children, but some may lack the dexterity or motor planning skills for signing. If you try signing without success, you may need to fall back on PECS or an AAC as a better core vehicle for communication.

Figure 10: Common sign language

CHAPTER 9

UNLOCKING BEHAVIORS: ESSENTIAL TIPS AND TOOLS FOR SUCCESS

My mother told me to learn something new daily; as a behavior therapist, my kids ensure I do just that. I have learned the best-laid plans never go as expected, and I must adjust on the fly. I will break down things I do as a behavior therapist that you might find to be helpful tips. I mainly use redirecting and my sense of humor to handle every situation.

Redirecting guides the child's behavior from undesirable or inappropriate to more appropriate or acceptable. It means interrupting behavior and directing the child's attention toward something positive. For example, if the child refuses to share, you might respond, "Let's find another toy we can all play with." Or if the child wanders away when you are out, say, "Let's go on a treasure hunt around the area and find objects." These are examples of redirecting the child from an undesirable behavior to a more appropriate and engaging activity.

Below are two examples from my experience where I identified the triggers and subsequently handled the situations.

• • •

I gave another behavior therapist (BT) a break and walked into the classroom to find crayons and markers scattered all over the floor and table. I asked the BT what happened. She replied, "We were just sitting here, and he got mad and threw the markers. I told him to clean up, and he threw the rest of the markers and crayons."

I responded. "Well, I guess I won't ask him to clean up then," and the child laughed.

I asked him if he wanted to talk, and he shook his head no.

I asked if he could draw instead, and he said yes. He drew three people, one of whom was big. I asked who the big person was, and he pointed at me.

I joked, "Boy, don't put me in your mess! I wasn't even here. Don't try to get me caught up."

He laughed. I then asked if the other character was the other BT, and he said yes. I asked about the other people in the drawing, and he said it was him and the kid sitting next to him.

I said, "Oh, so the BT wasn't paying any attention to you and was giving the other kid attention, and you didn't like it, so you threw the stuff on the floor?"

He said yes. I continued, "And then she asked you to clean up, and you didn't like that either?"

He said no, he didn't. Throughout our conversation, I pointed to the crayons and markers and then to the bin, and he put them back where they belonged.

I discovered the initial trigger was his need for attention from the BT, and the second trigger was being told to clean up. While gathering this information, I also managed to get him to clean up just by pointing to what I wanted him to do.

• • •

The child shut down, stopped working on his math, and walked out of the center. I started walking with him and asked what was wrong, but he didn't respond. I noticed he had drawn all over his arms.

I said, "Oh, look at that work you got on your arms! Who did that masterpiece? Did it hurt?"

He laughed, and I said, "That's some mighty fine scribble-scribble you got there; it's almost as good as mine. Would you like to see?"

He said yes. I told him, "Well, you have to turn around and start walking back to the center."

He agreed, and I showed him one of my tattoos as we walked back.

I then asked why he walked out of the center in the first place, and he said he was mad because there were too many math problems.

I said, "For each math problem you do, I can show you one of my tattoos." I thought to myself, *Phew, I'm glad I have a lot of tattoos.*

I told him we could do half the page now and half the page later, so it didn't seem like as much work. Once he finished the whole page, he could pick two tattoos from a pack to put on.

I discovered the trigger was too many math problems. I modified his work by breaking the work into halves and completing them at separate times. I got him safely back to the center and incentivized him to complete the work by showing him my tattoos.

• • •

Lastly, here are other helpful tips:

- If I'm working with kids and I already know what TV shows or music they like, I pre-set them on my phone using YouTube. When an outburst arises, I quickly access the preferred items and play them. It usually gains their attention and snaps them out of aggression.

- If you wear glasses, I recommend anti-slip ear grips. They help keep my glasses on during an outburst. They are cheap but very effective, and you can find them on Amazon or at a local optometrist's office.

- One often overlooked strategy is self-care. As a parent or caregiver, you must look out for yourself and find ways to decompress after moments of aggression or the daily grind of behavior. Joining support groups can provide the opportunity to talk to other parents who are in the same situation. Additionally, taking walks, listening to music, or simply having time to yourself can make a big difference. Remember, you are no good for your child if you are burned out or stressed. Take time for yourself, and don't get down on yourself if things don't get done that day. There is always tomorrow.

CONCLUSION: EMPOWERING THE CAREGIVER

This has been and will continue to be a long journey. The challenges will get easier as you gain the tools and knowledge needed to navigate the path. Understanding behavior is not about what a child says or does but the deeper motivation, function, and context that shape the behavior. Throughout the book, I have emphasized the importance of recognizing the behavior's function and triggers. Preventing behavior from occurring is aided by recognizing them earlier. I have provided practical strategies to help effectively address a wide range of behaviors.

Parents need to tailor strategies to their child's needs and circumstances. My most frequently used, most effective (perhaps surprisingly) strategy is simply saying, "No, thank you." I've found it catches children off guard, leading to a pause as they process my response. It's during this moment of hesitation that I swiftly redirect behavior. I can easily guide them toward a more appropriate behavior by interrupting their thought process.

This guidebook emphasizes the importance of building strong, trusting relationships with children through processing. Communication, empathy, and connection are key to building a meaningful relationship to guide behavior.

Parents, you can empower your children to thrive and reach their full potential. With the knowledge and strategies provided, you can embark on your journey with confidence and a deeper understanding of behavior. Remember, *you are the biggest advocate for your child and their needs*; never underestimate the power of unconditional love. It takes a village; you are not alone in this journey. Together, we navigate the ups and downs of behavior and celebrate victories.

I aim to ensure my strategies are affordable for you to implement on your own. I designed them to be practical and easy to incorporate into daily life. I want you to be able to effectively address behavior without the need for expensive resources or specialized training. At the end of this book, I have provided tracking sheets for collecting data to help you see which strategies work well and which don't. The pages are designed for you to make copies to retain for your records and provide to school administrators and healthcare providers. We're all part of the team, so if you discover a successful strategy, please share it with your support community.

The techniques and behavioral strategies you learned in this book should empower you to handle diverse behaviors with grace and efficacy. As a family support therapist at the Center for Autism and Related Disorders (CARD), I was frequently asked questions by my families. Subsequently, I sought resources to better support them. I gained information in my research that I now pass on to you. I strive to equip you with as many tools and resources as possible to ensure your toolbox is full.

A friend of mine has a son with severe nonverbal autism, and she has this to say about the importance of understanding behavior: "I think the mantra, 'Behavior is communication,' is the hardest and also the most valuable lesson I've learned from being an autism mom. It makes you so much better at life in general, knowing that truth in your relationships and daily interactions with all people."

My motivation in writing this book is empowering caregivers and sharing teaching tools to navigate the unpredictable journey of understanding and responding to behavior. I hope this fosters a feeling of love and trust in your home for all your family members.

HELPFUL RESOURCES

Autism Speaks
Grant applications for family assistance.
https://www.autismspeaks.org/autism-grants-families

Parent Center information & resources
Helps parents find coping resources and suggestions for partnering with schools.
https://www.parentcenterhub.org/behavior-athome/

Childcare.gov
Resources to assist you financially in providing for your child's needs.
https://childcare.gov/consumer-education/
understanding-and-responding-to-challenging-behaviors

Intensive Care For You
Offers behavior counseling and other free resources. Includes IEP goals, BIP forms, and activity schedules.
https://intensivecareforyou.com/resources-for-free/

Song of Love Foundation
A non-profit organization that creates custom songs for kids and teens facing medical, physical, and emotional challenges. They create professionally produced lyrics featuring the child's name and references his or her favorite things, with a performer singing it.
https://songsoflove.org/

Special Kids Photography of America (SKPA)
Families of kids with special needs who are stretched thin with medical or therapy bills may apply for a Smiles for Katie Family Photo Grant. You can receive a free photo shoot and 8 x 10 photos. The grant is named after a four-year-old with Down syndrome, Katie, who passed away while on vacation with her family. You can apply for the grant only if you work with an SKPA photographer.
https://www.heartsandlens.org/

Stop Bullying
This site has everything about different types of bullying and how to deal with the situation if it arises.
https://www.stopbullying.gov

Wings for Autism
A national program that allows individuals with autism (along with their families) to rehearse a plane flight, complete with obtaining boarding passes, going through security, and boarding a plane.
https://thearc.org/our-initiatives/travel/

The iTaalk Autism Foundation
Has an App Facilitator Program that provides kids with disabilities of all kinds with up to $250 in free apps per calendar year.
https://www.itaalk.org/#!app-facilitator-guidelines/cbls

Variety - the Children's Charity
Gifts manual and powered wheelchairs to children along with adaptive bikes, walkers, and other gait-assistance gear through local chapters.
https://usvariety.org/

Wheelchairs 4 Kids
Provides wheelchairs to children and can also assist with ramps, wheelchair lifts, and home modifications.
https://wheelchairs4kids.org/

If you have any questions about a behavior I didn't cover you can email me at spectrumprotection2@gmail.com and I will try and help.

DOCUMENTATION FORMS

MONTH: _____

Habit	1	2	3	4	5	6	7	8	9	10	11	12	13	14	15	16	17	18	19	20	21	22	23	24	25	26	27	28	29	30	31	Result
Use Timers																																
Visual Supports																																
Snacks (eating)																																
First/Then Board																																
Offer Breaks																																
Choices																																
Sensory accommodations																																
Breathing Exercises																																
Environmental Modifications																																
Priming																																
Break Task Into Smaller Steps																																
Notes:																																

OUTBURST TRACKER

Date:	Start Time:	Finish Time:

Duration::	Location:

Triggers:

What went well:	What actions were taken:

What Happened:

Strategies used:

medication tracker.

medication	dose	start	stop	side effects

PROCESSING

Draw, or write the answers to these questions
in each box..

What were you
feeling at the time?

What did you do?

How are you feeling
now?

What could you do
next time?

Who do you need to
apologize to?

www.ingramcontent.com/pod-product-compliance
Lightning Source LLC
Chambersburg PA
CBHW060351130626
46553CB00003B/1176

* 9 7 9 8 9 9 0 9 8 1 7 1 3 *